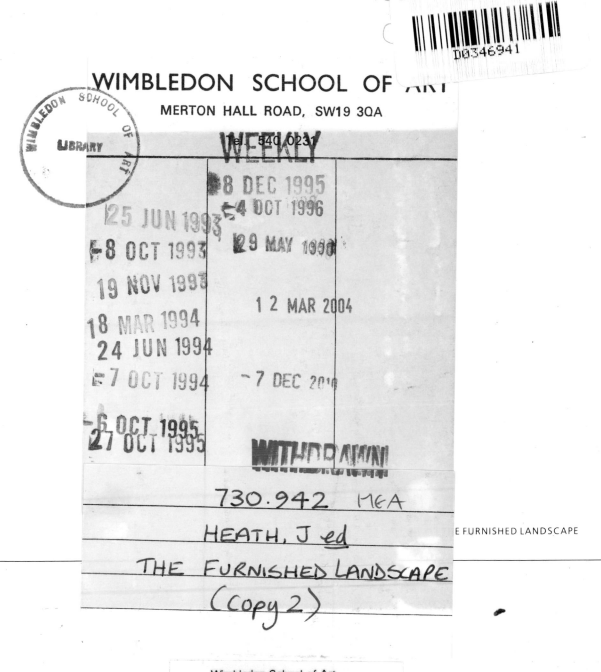

BELLEW PUBLISHING   CRAFTS COUNCIL AND THE ARTS COUNCIL

EDITED BY JANE HEATH

PATRICK NUTTGENS

FLORIS VAN DEN BROECKE

JANE HEATH

JOHN HOUSTON

THE FURNISHED LANDSCAPE : APPLIED ART IN PUBLIC PLACES

First published in Great Britain in 1992 by Bellew
Publishing Company Limited in collaboration with the
Crafts Council and the Arts Council

Bellew Publishing Company Limited
8 Balham Hill, London SW12 9EA

Copyright © Crafts Council/Arts Council/Patrick
Nuttgens/Floris van den Broecke/Jane Heath/John
Houston

Designed by Ray Carpenter

ISBN 1 85725 047 8

CONTENTS

ACKNOWLEDGEMENTS

RESEARCH FOR 'The Furnished Landscape' was guided by advice from public art agencies, Regional Arts Boards and Arts Councils throughout the country. The preparation of both book and exhibition has been dependent on the help given by numerous craftspeople and artists; art administrators and curators; planners and landscape designers. I would like to record my grateful thanks to all the individuals concerned for their thoughtful and generous contributions; as well as to members of the Crafts Council's Exhibitions Section; the Arts Council's Visual Arts Department; and to Adam Mills.

J.H.

FOREWORD

THE FURNISHED LANDSCAPE is about the contribution artists and craftspeople make in the design and fabrication of our public spaces, both urban and rural. The book seeks to encourage developers, planners, architects and other professions involved in commissioning landscape regeneration, that such collaborations carry a host of creative, economic and social benefits.

The Arts Council and the Crafts Council, together with other national and regional funding bodies, have been involved in promoting the commissioning of art and craftworks within building and landscape developments for some years but, in 1988, these bodies further endorsed this concept by accepting the 'percent for art' principle. This book, once again, reinforces our mutual commitment to this belief.

The book is published in conjunction with the Crafts Council's exhibition of the same title. Both explore and challenge the scope for works to be created beyond the normal perceptions of domestic or gallery situations, highlighting, in particular, the opportunities for larger works.

In addition, this book complements the recent Arts Council publication 'Percent for Art – A Review' and allows the consideration of other solutions to the enhancement of our environment.

Tony Ford
Director Crafts Council

Sandy Nairne
Director of Visual Arts,
Arts Council

March 1992

INTRODUCTION

THE FURNISHED LANDSCAPE sets out to draw attention to 'the gaps between buildings'. These pages map a new topography that is being drawn by artists and craftspeople in both town and country today.

The book takes a close-up look at applied art for public places – at the structures and detailed artefacts of landscape, the multifarious fixtures and fittings which can serve our practical needs and at the same time uplift and reassure, or divert us with decoration. Editor Jane Heath, curator of the Crafts Council's associated exhibition, argues that there is a rôle for today's artists and craftspeople as collaborators with other design professionals, breathing positive life into otherwise negative spaces; creating places "that affirm our sense of belonging or remind us where we are".

As a background to contemporary practice, Patrick Nuttgens traces development in landscape from the 18th century park to Modernism's structured spaces and beyond. He charts the ebb and flow of landscape artefacts – or 'gadgets' – more or less evident as the tangible, foreground expression of the changing aesthetics and philosophies of landscape design.

Where Patrick Nuttgens shows optimism about the future, looking to a "rebirth of visible ingenuity and invention", Floris van den Broecke's view is more circumspect. He examines the concerns of siting furniture in the contemporary landscape from his rigorous, close-up standpoint as a designer and maker of seating while bringing a European perspective to bear on his evaluation of practice in this country.

The subsequent sections focus on specific examples of ways in which contemporary British artists and craftspeople have responded to the challenge of applying their art to the landscape – of making artefacts which work and integrate with landscape design as a whole. This is a survey intended as the opening of a debate, not a summing up.

Jane Heath, with Isabel Vasseur, considers the scope for applied art in a central and formative rôle in landscape development – not as a finishing touch decorating the margins. The larger schemes cited reflect a firm, *ab initio* commitment on the part of the developing authority to this rôle, and show such commitment, often expressed in the form of a 'percent for art' policy, having far reaching results. But this section equally shows institutional planning informed, enhanced and complemented by the diverse ways in which people make their own creative mark on the places they use and care for.

The book concludes with John Houston's analytical profiles of a cross-section of makers and the work they have designed for landscape. Illuminating the stance each maker takes in their own field, Houston links their philosophies and working processes and sites their activity within the art/craft – and landscape – worlds.

The final Directory section offers some practical first steps for those wishing to act on the issues raised throughout the book.

'The Furnished Landscape' is a compilation of information and ideas, bringing together elements which are the outward signs of an inner awareness of the temporal fragility of landscape and our place in it; what Lawrence Durrell has called "the enduring faculty of self-expression inhering in landscape".

J.H.

THE MAKING OF LANDSCAPE PATRICK NUTTGENS

HOWEVER NATURAL and unaffected a place may look, the fact is that in our civilized world almost everything has been designed by someone. And that applies to spaces as well as to buildings, to rural and urban landscapes. Whatever its historical period, ancient, medieval, classical, Victorian or modern – or now post-modern – much of the landscape, and the most fundamental ideas enshrined in it, is man-made. And if that is true of the landscape as a whole, it is self-evidently true of the artefacts that go in it or with it: the items specifically designed for the landscape. These include all sorts of artefacts often taken for granted: boundaries, railings, fences, steps, seats, pavilions, play structures, letterboxes, telephone boxes, containers for plants and rubbish, stones, flags, bumps and holes and all the decoration that goes with them.

Borders hill farm with drystone wall, Southern Uplands. Photograph: Michael Wolshover

These are some of the items that, with many others, make up the totality of the landscape and therefore form a major component in its quality, as a work of art enshrining the expression and experience of the people who create it and use it and enjoy it. That applies to all periods and all countries; but to set a context for contemporary British landscape furnishings, it seems logical to start this appreciation by looking at one of the greatest and, certainly, the most recognizably national creative achievements of this country: the English landscape style.

England in the eighteenth century was in the midst of an agricultural revolution that involved nothing less than the transformation of the countryside. The landowners made a very beautiful land and created the great parks, with deer among the majestic trees. At a time when they enjoyed a life of as near perfect felicity as can be imagined, they could even, it seemed, perfect nature. And the professionals were there to help

OPPOSITE
West Sussex, Petworth House. Photograph: Visionbank/ England Scene

Lamp standards.
Photograph: Architectural
Association Library

London, the Embankment.
Photograph: Greater London
Records Office

them: Charles Bridgeman, William Kent, Lancelot Capability Brown, Humphrey Repton. And it was all wonderfully natural. Of Kent, it was said by a contemporary writer, "He leaped the fence and found all nature was a garden."

The technical discovery – attributed to Bridgeman – was the 'ha-ha' or sunken fence. One can hardly overemphasize what that meant. Because the fence was hidden in an excavated ditch, you could not see it; but it kept the cows away from the house, made the ground seem endless and Nature more natural than ever before. It was freedom. To the privileged owner sitting in his house, the view of a world apparently all his made him the monarch of all he surveyed.

But there was – out of sight and often out of mind – a massive catalogue of new artefacts used by an army of workers, making the whole environment possible. With the creation first of great lakes and then of a network of canals throughout the country, it was the first time absolutely straight horizontal lines appeared in the landscape. The apparatus that made that possible was – for the landowner – out of sight. For the worker and traveller it was very obvious: the dams, the aqueducts, the lock gates, the machines for raising water. It was "sweet concealment's magic art". In a calm and ordered environment, the observer could see unbounded sward, with clumps and belts of trees, bridges, fountains, temples and statuary – a wonderful man-made scene.

None of this was completely new. After all, Paradise had been a garden – the Garden of Eden – and against the background of the music and poetry of antiquity and its renaissance it must be possible to have Paradise regained and, better still, retained. The specially designed gadgets to make it possible – gates and fences and rocks and grottoes, both visible and hidden – would make the right magic. In a moonlit garden like Fountains or Studley Royal, with its succession of geometric lakes, its straight canals and its rising and falling paths, from one of which you could suddenly come across the 'surprise view' of the ruined abbey, the magic must have been almost tangible. But the apparatus for it was mostly – except for the people who knew the facts – wonderfully out of sight. For the working man it was a landscape which he had himself helped to make.

The time of change was the century which saw the triumph of an industrial revolution and a gradual but equally profound social revolution.

Bandstand and fountain, People's Park, halifax 44300

Halifax, People's Park: Bandstand and fountain. Photograph: Calderdale Amenities and Recreation Department

That was the nineteenth century, the Victorian age. It meant great houses, even larger and more elaborate than those of the eighteenth century, new farming methods and fishing fleets and the drastic growth of great industrial cities. In one city after another the working population was provided with parks, no longer surrounding great houses but in the middle of a town, like the People's Park in Halifax. While walking during sunset one evening near Mount Washington in the United States, Sir Francis Crossley had felt he "would like to be walking with my God on the earth. I said, 'What shall I render to my Lord for all his benefits to me?'" The answer was to render a park for his people in Halifax, so arranging art and nature that it would be within the walk of every working man, who might look over the banked-up edges to the beautiful hills behind.

There were great parks in Liverpool. The London parks – and in one major case its popular zoo – were celebrated. Once again, what made this possible was the invention and development of artefacts – gadgets now no longer hidden but part of the people's landscape. And there was such variety! Street furniture could be designed and made specifically for the place, plainer or more elaborate to express the pride of the city and its obvious technological achievement. And man-made artefacts were not the only beneficiaries of this development.

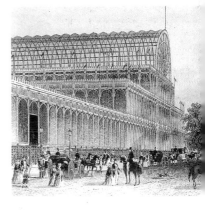

London, Crystal Palace: south transept, 1851. Photograph: Mary Evans Picture Library

13

A greater variety of colourful new plants, making the seasons more easily differentiated, were imported to add to the native specimens. The inventions were prodigious. The grass was controlled, no longer by cattle or sheep, but by lawnmowers. And the plants could be not only nurtured and moved but displayed for all in greenhouses. Greenhouses became major new components of the landscape – like the Great Stove at Chatsworth by Paxton – and were made glorious in the same Paxton's fantastic greenhouse, the Crystal Palace, erected for the Great Exhibition of 1851.

They were sometimes the dominant element of, sometimes the accompaniment to a catalogue of artefacts available for all – the bandstands and pools of the parks, statues available in artificial stone and cast iron (especially Queen Victoria who appeared in the centre of towns and villages as well as cities), seats and shelters, balusters and bridges, trellises for plants and fruit that could make a live growing wall, ever more fantastic graveyards which were also public parks, with gravestones in stone and artificial stone and cast iron, sometimes exuberant in invention like the Necropolis in Glasgow or Highgate in London. At the seaside, more popular with every year and made accessible through convenient transport, there were piers and towers and pavilions and machines. It was a world that required an army of workers and carers and it spread, like the social revolution, to all places on all scales – from the classic temples in Roundhay Park in Leeds to the gnomes that decorate the suburban houses in every city.

What transformed that popular scene was the international modern style of architecture and its effect upon almost every part of the environment. It was an international movement in that it spread everywhere and was intended explicitly to be common to all people, of every place and every level of prosperity. Illustrated books, travel on an unprecedented scale, scenes on film and television, made everyone aware of traditions different from our own, often more colourful and punctuated with different artefacts. But in terms of design, it meant the elimination of much of the detail of architecture and landscape. We might be better informed, but we were also likely to be less understanding.

The international style replaced detail by simple planes and inter-penetrating spaces; it was the architecture of space, rather than of style.

Kronforth Garden: landscape design by Roberto Burle Marx. Photograph: Landscape Institute Library

OPPOSITE
USA, Los Angeles: Storer House by Frank Lloyd Wright, 1924. Photograph: Arcaid Picture Library

And this was obviously true of the contemporary landscape. Of some of the supreme examples, two of the most influential were painters who turned their attention to landscape.

Roberto Burle Marx created astonishing new landscapes in Brazil by the use of luxuriant local flora with strong colours in huge abstract patterns, applying some of the discoveries of abstract painting to the emergent landscape. Earlier in England, Gertrude Jeckyll used big banks of planting so that the colours would succeed each other and provide a changing landscape that looked complete at any one time. She worked closely with Edwin Lutyens, who provided an equally inventive and apparently inexhaustible succession of architectural settings and artefacts, including benches for the garden. But possibly most influential on all designers in this field was Frank Lloyd Wright. His fantastic output of houses (he had designed over 140 by 1910) was only the first phase of his work. But in that first phase the 'prairie house' illustrated his deliberate attempt to eliminate unnecessary parts of the house and separate rooms and make it all come together as enclosed space, "so divided that light, air and vista permeated the whole with a sense of unity"; and that involved "associating the building with its site by extension and emphasis". Essential to its character was the interpenetration of interior and exterior spaces and shapes.

Glasgow, Necropolis.
Photograph: Valerie Bennett,
Architectural Association Slide
Library

What this all adds up to is a basic tenet of the modern movement in architecture and design – and that such design is ultimately concerned not with detail but with space, and particularly with a sequence of spaces, from interior to exterior. The components are planes and shapes, masses and lines, texture and colour. Colour came into its own in landscape in a way that it had not in the eighteenth century; Capability's universal landscapes were essentially monochrome – form without change of colour. It has been one of the discoveries of our time, shaped by the discoveries in colour and light of the Impressionists and Post-Impressionists, that those two elements were the very essence of form.

And even more so when we saw the environment as a totality subject to constant change. Some changes were caused by the technology of our own making; more were natural biological changes, about which we know more and of which we can be aware in an unprecedented way through film and photography and the microscopic revelation of organic growth and natural form.

All of this resulted in our paying too little attention to the man-made artefacts which are an integral part of the total environment. In fact there were more of them, some so large, like cooling towers, that they passed unnoticed by the majority of citizens, simply because they had become part of the daily scene. At good moments they were positive additions – like the telephone boxes designed by Giles Gilbert Scott, the architect of Liverpool Cathedral and Battersea Power Station. Their replacement by negative shelters rather than boxes may be more convenient for dogs needing relief, but it is a serious lapse in public quality.

Letterboxes are a part of the landscape everywhere; so are street lights and endless pylons; play structures are ingenious essential components of the public park; lettering itself sometimes becomes a major element in the design of the landscape, not only on motorways.

Mile marker, 19th Century.
Photograph: Michael Wolshover

If we argue that components of the modern landscape are an essential contributory part of the total design, can we define what part they play in the genesis of the design, as we could in many architectural periods? There have been moments when the design (and ultimately the perfection) of a component was the mainspring for a complete style. It can be argued, for example, that the development of the groin vault (seen first in an aisle of Durham Cathedral) created what came to be the Gothic style. It could be argued that the timber staircase of a great house was a key to the style of Jacobean architecture. It is generally accepted that the Georgian sash casement window is the most effective window ever created for this climate, and its total development was a key to the style of Georgian houses and towns. Designs for garden buildings could have a similar effect.

For the landscape architect or designer of today – a young profession that became official and independent only in 1929 – there now exists a wealth of gadgetry, as well as experience, that gives him or her a freedom that would have been astonishing to most earlier periods and their designers. This includes moving and replanting trees and shrubs, not perhaps on the arrogant scale of Louis XIV at Versailles, but more generally. We can choose furniture from catalogues, and create an almost instant landscape, as in the Garden Festivals of recent years. We must therefore ask: What are the components that can generate a modern landscape and what are its artefacts?

Fundamental, now as many times before, must be water, controlled

Scotland, Torness: Powerstation showing landscaping and agriculture.
Photograph: Michael Wolshover

London telephone box designed by Sir George Gilbert Scott, 1925.
Photograph: Architectural Association Slide Library

and exploited as lakes and pools, ice rinks and fountains of many shapes and sizes. If that is elemental, so are the basic landforms, man-made as well as natural; terraces, ramps, steps. Enclosures are fundamental to any functional landscape, both hard and soft. With this goes the design of protection, from heat and cold, wind and rain. The basic materials are the same as ever: land, grass, trees and shrubs. More evocative than before are the effects of colour and light; less evocative sometimes, except when the scale changes and they become dominant, are the objects in the landscape, from statues to cooling towers. But above all in the contemporary landscape are the people who use it, observe it and inevitably, by using it, change it.

What this essay has attempted to do is select some basic themes from a few periods, mainly but not wholly in England. The fact is that no landscape is purely national; whatever its local peculiarities, its influence spreads everywhere. And so do the objects that are part of the story.

In the last few years they have become, in sympathy with the style, quiet, restrained and sometimes almost invisible – hidden controls and functional containers so much taken for granted that they are unnoticed. Now the scene is changing again. We are seeing a rebirth of visible ingenuity and invention; and we expect to see more detail, more objects unnecessary as well as necessary, decorative as well as functional.

Leith, Edinburgh: street furniture.
Photograph: Michael Wolshover

Their variety is not yet enough; but it is increasing with every year.

The key to that change is design. It is a process in which many professionals take part, from architects and industrial designers, craftspeople and artists, furniture makers and decorators, to the manufacturers of mass-produced artefacts. It is followed by many people and its products concern everyone. Because they are everyday objects they have lots of different characteristics. In an age of pluralism, there is no one style, no one fashion, no one standard of beauty. But they are coming back: obelisks, columns, statues, sundials, urns and rocks. They are also fun. "If in doubt," said one of my architectural instructors many years ago, "you can always insert an urn."

Pot by Monica Young, 1991.
Unglazed stoneware,
145 × 100cms.
Photograph: Roger Murray

CIVIC AND SYLVAN SEATS

FLORIS VAN DEN BROECKE

I HAVE ALWAYS thought that landscape is the main inspiration for human creativity. Conversely, at least in the twentieth century, landscape is man's creation. The exigencies of survival and the need for shelter forged a seemingly unbreakable bond between man and his environment, in which the landscape relinquished its material and spiritual riches to the point of exhaustion. No sooner did any society triumph over the elements, than that society turned the tables on Nature and used the landscape for its trade and pleasure.

Of the many chattels and implements man has developed to accompany civilization and to expedite the development of complex societies, furniture is but a single – if crucial – element, one prevalent only in the last 3,000 or so years.

Made from materials ready to hand, but embellished for power with materials from afar, furniture has played its dual rôle as the moveable resting place for people and goods. As a branch of the applied and decorative arts, it has aspired to the heights of finer things; as part of the tradesman's stock, it has the humble function of billeting the bottom.

In industrialized society, furniture has become increasingly divorced from the art of building, but has retained its kinship with many other trades. Today's wheelwright and coachbuilder, the automobile manufacturer, counts the car seat as an intrinsic part of the product. The personal computer has engendered so-called ergodynamic operator's furniture so far removed from the carpenter's constructions that these objects hardly bear any relationship to the sticks and planks that were turned and adzed from the beech and elm of Wycombe's woods. Yet they remain basically tables and chairs. The craft of the cabinet maker himself

Stourhead, The Hermitage: carved stone bench.
Photograph: Edwin Smith

OPPOSITE
Milton Keynes Development Corporation: Wood slatted bench by Geoff Hollington, 1972. Hardwood slats, tubular steel. Photograph: Geoff Hollington

One of many versions of this industrial product found throughout Britain from parks to ports. A typically modernist design, it is reductivist but graceful, and in this setting at one with its environment.

Kent, Sissinghurst: Hardwood garden bench by Lutyens. Photograph: Neil Crawford

Private yet formal and like much outdoor furniture now in reproduction, Sir Edwin Lutyens' garden bench design for Sissinghurst is architecture on a small scale. It would be out of context anywhere else but in a garden.

can be imitated, with the precision of intentional imperfection. Where once the camera was a wooden case, now case furniture has photographed and imprinted woodgrain, invoking the landscape as its original source. Furniture abounds with such artifice.

The beneficial tension between the natural and man-made environment is a phenomenon greatly misunderstood by the creators of today's landscape. Worse still, it is almost entirely beyond the comprehension of the designers of townscapes. Man's potentially enriching contribution is frustrated on the one hand by the weedy pokiness and leaded 'tudorbethan' pedestrianization of town council and developer alike, and on the other by the brutal expansionism of the six-lane highway. It is true that the car seat has made the street bench redundant, but where the car does not go, there still follow its exhaust-pipe dreams. As with architecture, the machine aesthetic in the hands of second rate designers remains like machines out

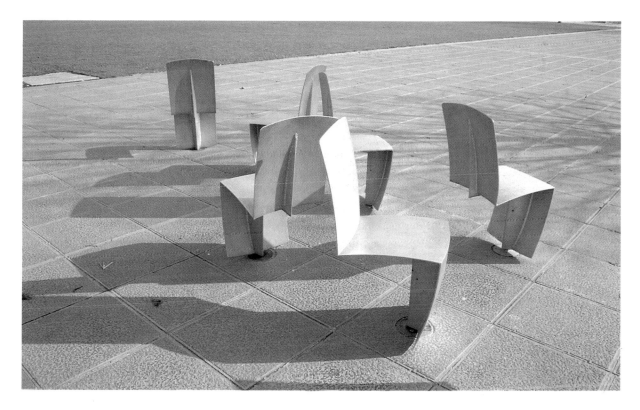

Paris, Parc de la Villette: Swivelling chairs designed by Philippe Starck, 1991. Cast aluminium mounted on pivot.
Photograph: Sara Bowler

As part of 'Le Grand Projet', the Parc de la Villette on the site of the former abbatoirs is a worthy twentieth-century addition to the parks of Paris. A wholly contemporary landscape, as much a science park as pleasure gardens.

of human control. Whereas the true builder and designer, who in England would be a gardener, hones the edge of the modern landscape more delicately.

Like any historical style, modernism has produced a plethora of furniture, but curiously little of distinction for outdoors. Furniture is usually thought of as something for indoors, at least in Britain, where, in any case, modern furniture hardly gained even a toehold behind the Englishman's front door. Outside his garden gate, both the rural and urban landscape remain a battlefield. Just about any public space with any graceful furniture seems to have been inherited from the confident and public-spirited Victorians, creators of the now archetypal park and station bench, later complemented by the classic garden and leisure furniture from the outdoor-minded Edwardians. While Europe was busy remodelling itself in the modern mould after her deflowering, English furniture

Barcelona, Guell Park: detail of mosaic by Antonio Gaudi, 1900–14. Ceramic mosiac laid on concrete.
Photographer: unknown

Walls become benches above grottos and footpaths. Antonio Gaudi's completely integrated vision makes no structural distinction between these functions.

Sofanco Bench by Oscar Tusquets, 1988. Terrazzo.
L.200cm, H.85cm.
Photograph: Lluis Casals

Transposed to the era of industrial production, one of Gaudi's heirs, Oscar Tusquets, wrought elegance from an otherwise unwieldy and formless material. This bench inherits and extends the tradition of the many public stone benches found in Spain.

quality, often advanced in favour of the crafts, becomes dubious when work fails in fundamental structural and finishing aspects, but is successful as a carrier of visual semiotics or pure aesthetics. Quality in such a case can be perceived only as a combination of its attributes. In any case, in both mass-production and handwork, the intrinsic labour and material value can be expressed only in monetary terms, just as the market value – arising either from artistic merit or rarity – can.

Even the more monolithic cast pieces are usually finished by hand. In the surprisingly graceful, and sometimes spectacular benches from the Barcelona firm Escofet, one sees a thorough exploitation of the material. Weighing up to 850 kilograms apiece, these benches could be seen as replacements of the hand-built ornamental benches seen around the squares and streets in Spain. Integration into the structural fabric of buildings follows a longstanding local tradition, reaching the high point in Antonio Gaudi's work. Here, the separation between a piece of furniture as a perceived moveable object and the building as an *immeuble* is completely erased.

When the traffic is ambulatory rather than vehicular, the pavement is more susceptible to this approach than the street. Bollards – which include in their ambivalent function that of keeping cars out or in, but at least separate them from the pedestrian – together with bins, lighting and planters, make up the bulk of landscape furniture catalogues and provide considerable scope for imagination. As a purely formal sculptural exercise (none the less redolent with civic symbolism), the new bollards down the Damrak in Amsterdam trace the tram ride from the Central Station to the Mint as boldly as a regiment of royal guards. Their perfect foil is found in the semi-public café terrace seating lining the pavement, alternately tidy and disordered and full of people. It is a townscape typical of a harmoniously functioning and vibrant, living city.

Visual and functional elements operate similarly in the rural environment, where scale and detail play off against each other. It is the furniture that provides the human scale against an architectural or natural background. Whereas the craftsperson can manipulate these factors to draw attention to the significance of the object being sited in a specific place, the products of industry have to be more general. Nevertheless, judicious design can impart that specialness which the incidental and

Festival of Britain 1951: Chairs by Ernest Race. Bent steel rod. Photograph: Gillian Naylor

The 1951 Festival of Britain stimulated industry, architecture and design. Later festivals have not had as much impact on designing for landscape in spite of valiant attempts.

unique so often appear to possess. In Parc de la Villette, a gigantic reurbanization scheme in Paris, Philippe Starck's randomly scattered semi-industrially produced pivoting chairs do just that. One imagines them to be out-of-space toadstools in a forest of trees, rather than in a forest of structural steel. One imagines that these objects, imbued as they are with candid primacy, are equal in measure to the power of Nature. In man's heroic effort humbly to seat a weary body, this seems a peculiarly twentieth-century enterprise. It leaves no room for the limp lumber encumbering our landscape and impels us to consider at least a contemporary, if not a visionary alternative, to the retro-repro so beloved of the wimpish and escapist landscaper. Preserve and restore what is there. But it is imperative, not only for the beautification of our present landscape, but also for our future one – and even more so for its very existence as a utility – that the freedom and responsibility which the practice of craft and design have bequeathed us hitherto as a benchmark have the strength to confront the millennium.

Seats by Rodney Kinsman. Cast aluminium and rolled steel on stone plinths. Photograph: RCA

Crystal Palace, another influential work carried out for a festival, the Great Exhibition of 1851 and designed by the gardener Joseph Paxton, is regarded as the precursor of British High-Tech architecture. The foremost modernist designer-manufacturer Rodney Kinsman evokes Paxton's creation in his tough transport seating.

City of Amsterdam, the Damrak:
Bollards by the Municipal Design
Department Street Furniture,
1991. Cast metal.
Photographs: Dienst Ruimtelijke
Ordening

*Bollards are a traditional element in
the streetscape of Amsterdam. No
longer used for mooring merchant
ships, they now keep cars from
falling into the canals. Along the
Damrak these bollards mark the
entry route from Central Station to
the Mint. As in Paris, enlightened
official patronage can enhance
the necessary changes in the townscape demanded by twentieth-
century needs.*

CHANGING PLACES

JANE HEATH

WITH ISABEL VASSEUR

WE ARE SURROUNDED by more and more culture, less and less nature. But while in Britain the value of open space as breathing space is fiercely defended, landscape in the popular imagination is usually the private domain of gardens, or a largely illusory idea of 'natural' countryside. There is little sense of a strong contemporary vision for our communal created spaces.

When we enter a building we enter owned territory. But streets, squares, parks, village greens and common land, seaside promenades, national parks – these are the places whose ownership we share, the places which we use and enjoy on equal terms and for which, however indirectly, we have responsibility. It is here that an outward expression of our civic and social lives is uniquely represented, and made to function more or less satisfactorily. It is here, too, that we look for the reassuring signs, often in the detail and the commonplace, that affirm our sense of belonging or remind us where we are.

What is the rôle of applied or practical art in helping to cultivate the often fragile attributes of image, identity and social function in public places? Considering the scale and complexity of contemporary land-scape making – the economics of development, the aspirations of client and designer, the demands of traffic and public safety, the seemingly unchallenged power of public utilities – can there be a creative space for artists and craftspeople to operate effectively, and centrally, in collabor-ation with landscape or other design professions? Or are artists to be called on at the last moment to decorate the margins?

The idea of siting sculpture as landmarks and signifiers has gained widespread currency in recent years. Sculpture has status. What is

Lewisham, Marischal Road: Bollard by John Maine, 1990. Cast iron, H.120cm. Commissioned by London Borough of Lewisham. Photograph: John Maine

OPPOSITE
Nottingham Town Hall: banners made by Maddi Nicholson and children from local coal mining communities in 1991. Com-missioned for Nottingham Festival and funded by British Coal. Each banner: 9m × 1.5m, painted in silk screen inks.
Photograph: Keith Tiddball

considered here are some of the often more subtle, open-ended, diffuse and flexible approaches possible via the imaginative application of art to the structures, textures, decorations and utilitarian furnishings of landscape.

Forty years ago, the Festival of Britain site was an open-air setting for art, both applied and fine. When the practice for new towns to employ Town Artists started at Peterlee, the painter Victor Pasmore worked on layout and landscaping. But Henry Moore took the 'high ground' with sculpture in landscape, and in Britain the dominant orthodoxy thus established for 'art in the environment' has perhaps only in recent years begun to be challenged.

When in 1986 Jim Partridge went to work as Craftsperson-in-Residence in Grizedale Forest, in the Lake District, he was the first 'non-sculptor' to contribute to the forest's innovative and influential Sculpture Project. It was a new departure for Partridge, too, furnishing outdoor spaces. He made a walkway and a bridge, unostentatious in themselves, but seminal works in his own development and in the opening up of ideas about practical art in landscape.

In a very different context, the interest of artists in functional forms was emerging in the USA as a distinct philosophy for a public art with "the most social-minded intentions" (Scott Burton). The idea of a 'serviceable' sculpture, operating below the threshold of perception as art, has been prominently formulated, notably by Scott Burton and Siah Armajani, as well as by Dan Graham, Dennis Adams and others.

Liverpool, Tate Gallery: seating by Scott Burton, 1988. Steel, copper and slate. Architect: James Stirling. Photograph: Tate Gallery, Liverpool

Singular Visions

The sculptor John Maine will leave his mark in Lewisham – carved, cast and rooted into the town centre, in material and substance likely to outlast many of the buildings which might more readily be taken as Lewisham's essential 'thereness.' Buildings are transient things compared with the matrices of road, river and railway to which they cling; and it is to these bones of the landscape that Maine has applied his art.

Maine's part as a member, from the outset, of the Lewisham 2000 Design Team undertaking a comprehensive redevelopment of the town centre, has allowed him to approach, in his words, "the whole project as a

OPPOSITE
Lewisham Town Centre, Ravensbourne Bridge: drawing for end post and section of railing by John Maine, 1991. Commissioned by London Borough of Lewisham.

Seattle, National Oceanic and
Atmospheric Administration:
Viewpoint by Scott Burton, 1983.
Terraced promontory, exposed
aggregate and steel.
Photographer: unknown

OPPOSITE
Swansea, Maritime Quarter:
Copper Flame seat and monument
designed by Robin Campbell
1985—88. Copper weathervane
and cap by Theo Gruneveldt and
Andrew Rowe, ceramic panels
designed and made by Martin
Williams. Commissioned by
Swansea City Council.
Photograph: Robin Campbell

London, South Bank Centre: *Arena*
by John Maine, 1983—88. Portland
stone, 122 × 1829 ×1829cms.
Commissioned by Arts Council
Photograph: John Maine

work of art . . . . The various objects and materials which make up the urban fabric may all become elements of a broader composition." The objects on which Maine has focused his own direct production are the central reservation of a dual carriageway, a massive quarter-mile-long carved stone barrier; bollards, posts, railings and a fretwork bridge parapet.

While Artist-in-Residence at the Yorkshire Sculpture Park during 1978–80, John Maine responded to the man-made elements "set in this landscape with real understanding . . . Bretton Park's gaunt sandstone gateposts greatly exceed the minimal function of supporting a gate. The varied wrought-iron fences, stone-clad gulleys and simple bridges . . . metal, wood, brick, stone and water are all seen here in positive rôles. . . . Awareness of structure and site combine with a sense of daring and feeling for the improbable."

There is a contained intensity about a dense row of Maine's cast iron bollards lining a Lewisham side street. They are unequivocally of our time, but not self-consciously so. Elsewhere, significant sites, distilled out of prolonged background work, serve as starting points for his series of objects, his characteristic 'phenomena', making visual connections throughout the town centre. Families of forms allow for recognition without repetition. The strategy is one of presence and focus, rather than a vain attempt at assertion over the visual cacophony of the High Street.

Maine's work combines a modernist exploration of pure form with a relish for the specific qualities of materials and making processes. He has applied, more than adapted, his art to Lewisham. In the give and take between artist and setting, some artists may seem to mediate and reaffirm the given identity of places, some may redefine identity through the strength and distinctiveness of their own work.

The seafront of Swansea's Maritime Quarter is a surprising place. Its elegantly designed promenade – no clutter of seats, no litter bins – is punctuated by a series of decorations and monuments. There are inscriptions, relief carvings, pavilions, a sundial and sculptures, their robust material presences not quite at ease with the rather insubstantial, all-new architecture; but they enrich the place with layers of meaning and reward the passer-by with a wealth of often enigmatic references that range through classical mythology, local history and natural phenomena.

The inspiration of the city which 'does not tell its past, but contains it like the lines of a hand, written in the corners of the streets, the gratings of the windows . . . every segment marked in turn with scratches, indentations, scrolls' (Italo Calvino's *Invisible Cities*) is acknowledged here. But this series of more than sixty 'enhancements' lacks the patina of time. Notwithstanding their hybrid eclecticism, these works were made possible by local planning conditions and realized within a space of ten years by the creative energy of Swansea City Council's urban designer, Robin Campbell. This is his vision materialized through resourceful collaborations with architects, artists and craftspeople as builders, stone carvers, letter cutters, sculptors.

The design of Swansea's city centre pedestrianization comes from a longer-term collaboration between Campbell and town artist Brenda Oakes. Like Tess Jaray's 'set-piece' city-centre designs for Birmingham and Wakefield (layout, paving and all furniture), theirs is an exercise in creating a unified and unique design identity. A Celtic-derived spiral motif built into paving patterns and furniture – seats, bollards, bins, planters, signposts – is special to Swansea. It remains to be seen how well the painstaking effort to achieve consistent quality, to the last detail, can withstand the onslaught of careless urban clutter, or indeed the impulse of shopkeepers and citizens to add their own more idiosyncratic contributions.

The Sum of Parts

"The richness and meaning of a place derives not from single items but from details which, taken together, contribute to a mosaic greater than the sum of its parts"

Peter Randall Page: Report on Castle Park for Bristol City Council, 1990

Bristol's Castle Park is a dramatic thirteen-acre central riverside site opened up by Second World War bombing. Preserved from commercial development, it was otherwise left for many years in a state of semi-neglect. Design for its refurbishment posed particular questions, the past being so insistently present both physically and in emotional associations. Finding no model in new city-centre parks elsewhere, it was decided to

Birmingham Centenary Square: paving designed by Tess Jaray in collaboration with Birmingham City Architects Department, 1989–1991. Commission organised by Public Art Commissions Agency. Photograph: Marriane Morris

take the place, its history and its interpretation, as the unifying theme for renewal.

Art and craft, though introduced too late to affect the overall park design, is an important ingredient of this pragmatic approach and a 'collection' of artworks will serve as signifiers and points of focus. Craftspeople, many from the West Country, provide the majority of the furniture, meeting practical constraints in terms of cost as well as function. The exploration of contemporary forms through hand-making in traditional materials keeps faith with both the present and the past. From forged iron railings fitting to historic remains, to light-weight litter baskets for summer use, there is scope for special commissions to turn awkward design problems into imaginative and enjoyable solutions.

As a central site with a working and shopping but not a resident community, Castle Park nevertheless aims to involve local people in its development and long-term 'ownership'. Whether through public consultations or workshops with commissioned artists, many Bristolians will in the course of time make their own mark on the place. Fittingly for a growing landscape, the development of the park is seen as ongoing, not

Gwynedd, Vale of Festiniog, Coed Cymerau-isaf: *Oak Leaf* seat by Howard Bowcott. Oak with stone plinth, 244cm×91.5cm×91.5cm. Commissioned by The Woodland Trust. Photograph: Martin Roberts

to be complete at any definitive moment. Changing events, such as a sequence of banner commissions, underline its nature as a living entity, as well as somewhere to be relaxed and amused.

Canary Wharf in London being the world's biggest commercial development, there is perhaps a certain irony that it should turn to the individuality of one-off and hand-made furnishings for its lavishly appointed public spaces. It is of course the very scale of the project which creates the need for humanization, or a 'non-corporate' style, and the benches, railings and other specially designed detailing fulfil their foreground rôle with elegance and vitality.

A generous proportion of the overall area is landscaped, intended by the developer Olympia & York to 'revive London's great tradition of public spaces in relation to architecture'. In terms of specially made street

OPPOSITE
London, Canary Wharf: Bench by Wales and Wales, 1991. Indonesian Teak from managed woodlands. L.244cm. Commissioned by Olympia and York, Canary Wharf Ltd. Photograph: Courtesy Olympia and York

furniture this constitutes a high-profile exercise in design within a distinct urban landscape convention; and a rare opportunity for the commissioned makers to demonstrate the levels of quality and impact of which they are capable.

The commissioning of seats by the Woodland Trust could hardly be in greater contrast. Instigated by a private legacy, the commissions form a series only from an organizational perspective. In a dozen woods around the country, a seat is encountered as an isolated artefact in woodland otherwise left as untouched as possible. The sufficiency of places of natural beauty challenges the artist's confidence to be discreet. The Woodland Trust, without a brief for the arts as such, has nurtured some of the most worthwhile experiments in this vein by artists and craftspeople, who have extended their own vocabularies in the search to parallel, in a piece of furniture, the spectacular inevitability of a tree.

Serendipity and Diversity

The character of most of our informal public landscape derives from gradual and piecemeal evolution. Artefacts in the past were unconsciously unified by the use of local materials, and forms refined by custom. Individuality and idiosyncrasy could find expression in gates and barriers, water troughs, milestones and signposts. Today the piecemeal approach in landscape artefacts widely persists, but on the whole the conditions for organic development, natural cohesion, local distinctiveness and the individual voice do not.

One exception is at North Shields. A steep bank above the Fish Quay with a sweeping view of the Tyne reveals unexpected detail – a miscellany of railing finials. The still-growing collection of fifty or so different 'nobbles' (as they are affectionately known) are fixed to pre-designed railings and enliven a spot re-landscaped with a sense of serendipity rather than unified planning. They are made at Newcastle Polytechnic as a collective enterprise in which students and staff of the sculpture department participate on equal terms.

The North Shields Fish Quay regeneration owes much of its special character to the presence of Free Form Arts Trust, an artists' group which has long helped people to make their own communal spaces –

playgrounds, gardens, streets – work better for them. This participatory approach creates places meaningful to their immediate users, and is an important route to successful commissioning. Its adoption for large scale and formal sites is seen in the Royal Free Square housing development in Islington, London, and at St Thomas's Peace Garden in Birmingham – two schemes where groups have joined with artists in planning, designing and making, in an endeavour to reinterpret the decorative rôle of metal street railings.

Photograph: Nick Blacknell

The Urban Design Group's criteria for 'The Good City' include "the opportunity for people to personalize their own surroundings; an environment should provide . . . public spaces robust enough to accommodate changes by their users". Banners belong to a tradition of community expression and protest. Though – or because – a temporary form, banner-making is an exuberant and relatively uninhibited way for groups and individuals to announce their presence and their feelings. "People animate places with pageant and make memories" (Sue Clifford *Common Ground*).

Ways of expressing contemporary cultural diversity in street furnishing have as yet hardly been explored. Prominent exceptions are the ornate structures which unmistakably mark the Chinese quarter in London and Manchester. In Smethwick, as part of the High Street improvement scheme in 1987, Sandwell Town Artist Francis Gomila worked with shop owners over six months to develop façade decorations projecting the colour, richness and authenticity of the commercial life whose specialized character now vividly reanimates the exterior as well as the interior of an Edwardian terrace.

North Shields, Fish Quay: finials designed and produced by Sculpture Department, Newcastle Polytechnic, 1990–2. Lost wax cast bronze, Diam. 10cm. Commissioned by North Tyneside Council. Photograph: Jane Heath

House fronts, gardens and shop fronts enclose the public landscape and perhaps shape its character more than any other factor. The extent to which individuals also contribute directly within the public domain may perhaps be underrated (leaving aside the obvious negative effects of vandalism). Village signs are a common example of intervention on a small scale, while in our streets, parks and countryside innumerable seats commemorate once favourite walks, views or resting places. The country churchyard, described by Robert Harbison as 'the model for a ground imbued with meaning', is finally a place for considered contribution to the communal landscape.

Birmingham, Smethwick High
Street: Francis Gomila in design
discussion with shop owners.
Photographer: unknown

Conclusion

There is scarcely any part of our managed environment which lies out-side the sphere of landscape design. Landscape designers deal in the abstraction of spaces – spaces which are at best recognized as at the heart of our public or social lives; or at worst regarded as no more than the gaps between buildings. Landscape designers are practised collaborators, working with the unpredictabilities of nature and the constantly unfolding drama of city streets. They are increasingly open to collaborations with artists and craftspeople. Together with the more permanent settings, the five national garden festivals between 1984 and 1992, successors to the Festival of Britain, have been an influential testing ground.

As a lesson in the creation of a total, expressive work of landscape art using modest parts and unspectacular craft skills, Sir Geoffrey Jellicoe's Kennedy Memorial at Runnymede still has relevance almost thirty years after its completion. His brief was to create a place and not a monument. In catalogue terms, the memorial consists of a wicket gate, a stone sett path, steps, an inscribed stone and two stone seats. These modest materials furnish an acre of land, an uphill climb, the sound of trees, a view – a message and a memory – a spirit of place renewed.

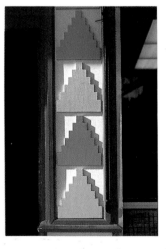

Birmingham,
Smethwick High Street
1987
All Commissioned by
Sandwell Metropolitan
Borough Council.
Photographs:
Francis Gomila

Detail of Billingham Shoes front
pilaster by Francis Gomila.
Cut and painted plywood.

Detail of Jalandhar Sweet Centre
front pilaster by Francis Gomila.
Cut and painted plywood.

Henna Stencil by Francis Gomila.
Emulsion paint stencilled
onto concrete render.

MAKING THE DIFFERENCE JOHN HOUSTON

THE FURNISHED LANDSCAPE of the late twentieth century is loud with signs and messages. In Britain this landscape is very like a living room: tidied up for special events, such as garden festivals; a bit more space cleared for bright new objects; regretful desires for the ones that got spoilt by use or neglect.

This section considers some makers and their recent projects. Modernism, in its Late and sometimes reviving mode, is the principal language, but how differently used by Richard La Trobe-Bateman to construct a bridge, and Marc Camille Chaimowicz to construct a garden artefact. Yet both are Modernist arguments.

George Carter's 'Noah's Ark' has reference to the centuries when important gardens were a complex kind of intellectual ordering, a synthesis of arts and sciences. This was a part of the huge social project we call the Enlightenment; its consequences include Modernism. In between ran the rocky rivulet of the Picturesque, later to flow into the torrents of the Romantic Movement. But at the junction of the eighteenth and nineteenth centuries the Picturesque rearranged Nature in terms of rough-hewn bridges and wayside seats "in perfect harmony with the wild but pleasing horrors of the scene". We still respond to similar harmonies; in this section they are interpreted by Jim Partridge and Liz Walmsley.

Plenty of other examples that are not so clearly titled are concerned with place. Enriching, adapting and marking particular places; placing objects to identify sites; reworking whole sites as a single entity.

One theme for the other voices: where the artefacts are drenched with meanings beyond themselves, they need to employ other voices, cite authorities. So it is with the words uttered in the work of Ian Hamilton Finlay, and in the work of Richard Kindersley.

OPPOSITE
Cumbria, Grizedale Forest:
Walkway by Jim Partridge and Liz Walmsley, 1986. Oak, 6m raised decking with 35m handrail. Commissioned by The Grizedale Society with Northern Arts Photograph: James Ravilious

Gateshead, National Garden Festival: Three steel bowls by Amanda Snow, 1990. Mild steel with bronze and graphite enamelled coating. Commissioned by 'Festival Landmarks' National Garden Festival 1990 Ltd. Photograph: Harriet McDougall

Hackney, Lea Valley Park Nature Reserve: *Rise and Shine* magic fish by Kate Malone, 1990. 'T' material set on railway sleepers. Commissioned by Lea Valley Parks Authority, managed by Public Art Development Trust. Photograph: Karen Robinson

MONICA YOUNG, AMANDA SNOW, KATE MALONE The asymmetric stance of Monica Young's big ceramics, their pale tone, warm, matt colour and a wavelike flexing of form, this all adds up to a statuesque presence – even though there is no image, just a very tall pot. But the near-human scale challenges our perception; as though our gaze is being met. The relationship is shaped by equivalence, by bodily empathy, by that ancient creation myth, still lurking in our culture, which interprets fired clay as living flesh.

Such explanations have several layers. Her urge to make each object as tall as her kiln resulted in unevenly fired glazes. Now she fires her pots without glaze; only burnt earth – terra cotta – unclothed. How do they fit the landscape? Her pots close vistas, guard terraces, act as focal points in clouds of foliage.

Amanda Snow relishes the craftsmanship of old machinery: the way they were made; the ways that they made other things. Her artefacts exist as bold forms, such as these hemispheres, which are embraced by precise elements of movement and articulation – the distinctive mechanical powers. Ruskin looked doubtfully for "the real dignity of mechanical Arts" but marvelled at the "assemblage of accurate and mighty faculties in them". Her large, active-looking steel bowls are a heroic mix of industrial hopper and classical urn. Recent work, in wood and glass as well as metal, is more mechanically complex: a huge clock; snakelike lights that invite manipulation; the Industrial Revolution as a decorative drama.

'Rise and Shine' is the title of Kate Malone's group of outsize freshwater fish, a brilliantly coloured, glittering ceramic surprise in the middle of a shallow lake in Hackney. They are the most idiosyncratic part of this subtly landscaped nature reserve recently established by the Lea Valley Park Authority in London. The lake was created from several old filter beds. She considers her objects as one of the many layers of material that visitors can discover there; these bright images of Nature, by a human creature, she suggests, are magical evidence of our nature.

Her stay in the nearby Homerton Hospital led on to the 'Optimistic Jug' now installed there. It is overflowing, with imagery and a perpetual welling flow of water washing down its sides. It is an image of plenty, of renewal, of hope; some more of the sympathetic magic which she believes objects can transmit.

Tall Urn by Monica Young, 1991.
Unglazed crank clay, H.146cm,
Diam.64cm. Photograph: Roger Murray

Water of Leith Walkway, footpath
next to River Leith: example of
pavingstone with incised lettering
by Richard Kindersley, 1991.
Hard York stone, each block:
59cm × 110cm
Photograph: Richard Kindersley

London, National Gallery,
Sainsbury Wing: Letterwork
designed and carved by Michael
Harvey with Annet Stirling and
Brenda Berman, 'Incisive
Letterwork', 1990–91. French
limestone, letters H.500mm.
Commissioned by National Gallery
and Robert Venturi.
Photograph: Michael Harvey

OPPOSITE
Glasgow, River Clyde Bridge:
Inscription: Ian Hamilton Finlay
with Annet Stirling and Brenda
Berman, 'Incisive Letterwork',
1990. Commissioned by TSWA
Four Cities Project.
Photograph: Richard Learoyd

RICHARD KINDERSLEY, INCISIVE LETTERWORK   The
lettering of Richard Kindersley is a very special part of the 'Water of
Leith Walkway', a scheme of refurbishment that has revived use and
occupation of buildings alongside this little river that leads out from
Edinburgh to its port of Leith. As the properties have been occupied,
their owners have helped with the costs of works on the walkway through
the Edinburgh organization 'Art in Partnership'.

Kindersley's project was concerned with poetry by two local men: a
shipwright, whose salty vernacular verse has been cut into the hard York
stone in a letterform based on beaten, hammered forms; and Robert Louis
Stevenson, whose poem of sea and rain was incised in letters based on the
slanting streaks made by the first drops of rain blown across a stone slab.
These few lines of poetry were also set out in a spiral – the whole project,
involving six big but different-sized stones set in the path, being gently
treated in what Kindersley refers to as a spirit of "visual onomatopoeia".
He helped to choose the site, at a bend in the river where there is a bench
to help the slower process of musing upon these inscriptions.

'Incisive Letterwork' is the partnership of Annet Stirling and Brenda
Berman, sometimes working for, and with, other letterers and artists.
They both worked with Michael Harvey on the lettering he designed for
the London National Gallery extension. The bridge, shown here, part of
the 'Four Cities Project', is over the River Clyde. Ian Hamilton Finlay was
the artist, proposing the idea and choosing Plato's words "All greatness
stands firm in the storm", to be carved in English and Greek. They had
worked with Hamilton Finlay several times before and the negotiating
between form and concept worked well again. But the bridge's granite pier
proved too durable and they had to adjust their design so that another
mason could cut it with power tools. It looks, they proudly say, as though
it had always been there.

Both partners teach this substantial and reviving art at the City and
Guilds of London Art School. Interested in many letterforms beyond
their beloved Roman, their recent work includes Gujarati and Hindi
inscriptions. Not wishing to offer any large generalizations, or to
philosophize, one partner mildly recommended their advice – on things
not to say in such a permanent form.

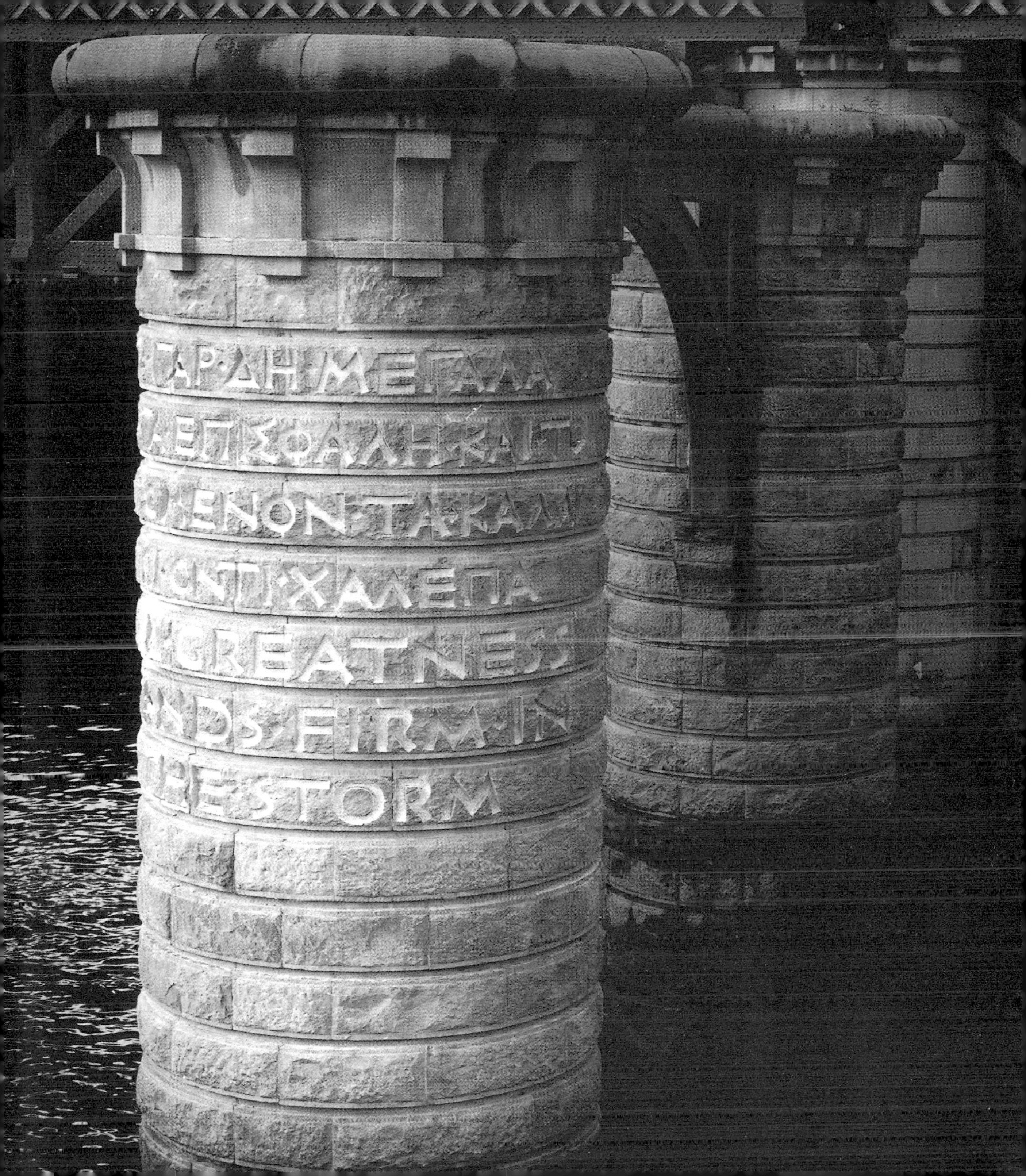
GREATNESS
DS·FIRM·IN
E·STORM

JIM PARTRIDGE AND LIZ WALMSLEY

Their work is thoughtfully untheoretical. As makers of wooden seats and bridges, fences and entrances, which have an inescapable – art presence (at least for present-day commissioners and admirers), they are wary of over-intellectualizing their own working processes. Immersed in those processes, their straightforward description of just what they do is cheerfully ingenuous, implying that their interventions into landscape are part of the fundamental activity of pathfinding and bridgebuilding. Their artefacts are complex signs: part monument, part celebration of Nature (its bounty of materials and metaphors) part trailblazing.

Discussing their little footbridge and other work on the thirty-nine-acre Ardtornish Estate, Partridge and Walmsley emphasized the unmadeness of this West Highland setting: all the vistas are out to sea; lots of little burns running through. Their task, as they saw it, was to create focal points and provide directional clues for newcomers . . . They were pathfinders too. Their accumulation of sites to work on added up to a rambling circuit of the estate through a full experience of terrain and artefact. In fact, most of their decisions are formed on site, often with the 'found' materials provided by the great gales of recent years. A search for fallen timber can discover the perfect site for a bridge; the peculiar needs of a seat or a fence can start a new search. They make much use of limbs with forks and elbows, seeking ready-made boughs for specific spans and drawing their 'designs' which only exist as conversation, on to the wood with blackboard chalk. They cut and prepare their green (unseasoned) timber with a chainsaw, always sawing along the growth. The drying wood will twist and writhe, but their construction allows for this. Using such windfalls also makes them braver about cutting green oak at £5 a ton, than working seasoned oak at £40 a foot.

But, back to theory: the origin of such sign-making, trailblazing work in the British landscape, was a polemical poem, 'The Landscape' of 1794–5, by Richard Payne Knight. From this very quickly came the theory of the Picturesque; at first it dealt with what was paintable in the wild Romantic landscapes of current taste. But soon the appropriate bridges made from fallen trees, and seats camouflaged as stumps, were actually being installed on Picturesque estates . . .

OPPOSITE
Argyll, Ardtornish Estate: footbridge by Jim Partridge and Liz Walmsley, 1990. Unseasoned oak, L:200cm. Commissioned by the Raven Family.
Photograph: Jim Partridge

ELIZABETH MCFALL, PAUL MASON   Two big new mosaic pavings in Arbroath by Elizabeth McFall refer to the textile history of this east-coast Scottish port: canvas for America's covered wagons, sails for Nelson's fleet. Her earlier installation at the 1990 Gateshead Garden Festival had used about two thousand metres of Arbroath canvas which had been made on century-old machines.

Her mosaics are based on altered images of a magnified weave. The scheme of dark greys, browns and whites blends with the basic paving blocks of the newly pedestrianized site. This unified ground smooths transitions and also helps to make sense of the deliberated gaps in her weave structure, which are encouragements to 'look through', beyond the weave, into an implied historic base.

Her generalized symbolism offers what she strongly feels is much-needed public pattern; it is site-specific and it fits local events, but not so specifically as to be only a badge or superficial sign. She speaks admiringly of Moorish tilework, of how it reads well as pattern even before the symbolism is understood; and so it may be in Arbroath, where her pavements can also be read as universal signs of an ancient activity.

Sheffield's Tudor Square is a quiet allegory of communication. Part of its meaning is defined by the uses of the surrounding buildings; the Crucible, Lyceum and Library theatres, the Graves Art Gallery and the Central Library. The old 1840s School of Arts and Crafts is now the Ruskin Gallery. In the middle of this, the square has been transformed from a car park to areas for performance, for sculpture, for seeing such events, and just for being there. Paul Mason, appointed as lead artist by the City Council, as part of the 'Percent for art' scheme, researched the culture of meaningful marks. Out of pictograms, ideograms, alphabets and conventional signs he constructed an interpretative synthesis of mark-making, a union of drawing and writing. Throughout the square there are signs: carved in stone, formed in forged steel, traced in long sweeps of mosaic (these last designed by Sue Mason).

These signs flow through the square, singly on the different-sized stones that form a principal feature as two long, curved walls; on railings, the signs form a long sequence; on the grilles round the base of trees, they are fitted all together into frames, like stencils for a universal message. Which is what they are.

Dundee, Ferguson Street: tile mosaic by Elizabeth McFall, 1988. Commissioned by Dundee District Council.
Photograph: Elizabeth McFall

Arbroath, Kirk Square: tile mosaic by Elizabeth McFall, 1991. Commissioned by the Arbroath Project.
Photograph: Elizabeth McFall

FLORIS VAN DEN BROECKE   In how many ways the Modernist project continues: as dream, faith, poetry; as space, measured by hope; as material experience, setting out again on the ideal path. Floris van den Broecke: painter become furniture designer, now Professor of Furniture Design at the Royal College of Art in London. Describing himself as a Late Modernist, discussing the nature of his thoughts about design, the continuities were wonderfully balanced – accounted for – against his own experience.

Two schemes: the first an inner courtyard in the Netherlands, defined by glazed façades. Dark glass, square white grids within square elevations – a systematic canon implying further cuboid spaces. This is 1982. His furniture fills the court with slanting rectangles of individual chairs – like an ordered structure randomly disposed, like a splintering ice-floe. In spite of being compatible, his chairs seem to propose alternative structures. Second scheme: commissioned for the 1990 National Garden Festival in England. These seats are wide enough for two, maybe three, persons on a grooved and curved polyester surface which is supported on a steel frame. The curves are subtle and informal, suggesting the hang and flow of a carpet thrown over a stepped form. As in the earlier scheme, planned and seemingly random elements co-exist; the inconspicuous frame establishes a delicate stance for the whole seat, but the upper surface appears dematerialized. As van den Broecke says in his Late Modernist mode, "The image has to be floated away." In fact, like a magic carpet, or a sheet of paper floating on top of a groundswell, this whole top form appears to be moving. The wavelike surface implies a continuous motion that seems to pulse through each form. But the apparent movement is quite slow, because the eye senses the braking effect of the rectangular grid beneath.

Van den Broecke, ex-painter, ex-rock-climber, talks about the ability to walk the ground and develop the eye to suit oneself. The working situation depends on the brief, but the earth is the starting point.

Sheffield, Tudor Square: mosaic
inserted into paving by Sue Mason
with Paul Mason, 1991. Marble
in stainless steel trays (one of
sixteen). Commissioned by
Sheffield City Council.
Photograph: Stuart Blackwood

OPPOSITE
Netherlands, Leeuwarden,
Giro HQ: seats by Floris van den
Broecke, 1982. Glass reinforced
cement. Commissioned by PTT,
Netherlands.
Photographer: unknown

MARC CAMILLE CHAIMOWICZ Ditchburn Place in Cambridge is a new housing scheme which fits sympathetically into a well-restored area of modest domestic dwellings built in the last two centuries. The long walk-through public garden in front of the scheme was developed at the same time, taking account of local suggestions, by the City Council. This water feature, designed by Chaimowicz in collaboration with landscape architect Douglas Rule, was made possible by assistance from the Eastern Arts Association via their 'Art in Public Places' scheme.

Chaimowicz, in his own words, "intentionally celebrated and upheld Modernist principles . . . [and] articulated my argument in COUNTERPOINT to the site". His argument was stated in what he (and others) call "the three noble materials of our century – glass, steel, concrete". All this was most definitely argument, and very far from the ornament that local people, who are the garden's principal visitors, seem to have expected. Water is featured: descending the levels in the central curved concrete ramp, and running down the curtain wall of tall glass slats which frames and embraces the ramp. A steel and concrete seat faces these elements and extends the argument in terms of forms and hierarchy and transparency. The whole project, with planting around and growth up and over the curtain wall, is a highly integrated scheme; in terms of concept and materials there is an extraordinary degree of refinement. It is, quite literally (and in a number of other ways) a spectacular argument – that is – its argument about Modernist principles is manifest as spectacle, although that mode of presentation has been interpreted in terms of delicate, domestic scale. The project is highly visible. Its built surroundings, new as well as refurbished, are brick and iron, tile and wood, gravel and paving; new construction, new proportions have been mildly camouflaged in a spirit of neighbourly consensus. Chaimowicz's scheme makes visible one or two things we all know about the twentieth century. Once, they were fierce beliefs (still are, for some), now they are enshrined in our lives and houses as assumptions (things you do not know that you know) and such eloquent advocacy can seem, paradoxically, to question the consensus.

That it was a real argument, and not merely a matter of Taste, was demonstrated in Chaimowicz's next landscape project. Invited by the architects of a new and very Modernist building, his designs are based on traditional rammed-earth techniques.

GEORGE CARTER   A classicizing 'Noah's Ark' for a children's hospital? Such clear formal references seem wonderfully odd in a book where the majority voice is Modernist, and the implied rhetoric mingles functional needs and vaguer emotional concerns. George Carter's concerns are much more crisply expressed, partly because his approach is so formal, and partly because his admiration is for artefacts in garden settings where Nature has been organized by Man. He is no Historicist – not interested in the process of reusing old images – but declares his affinity with the making of those seventeenth-century gardens which were a synthesis of the arts and sciences: involving architects, sculptors, hydraulic engineers and astronomers. The organization of space was drenched with different ideas; the articulation of form, for all the regard for precedents, was inventive, coherent and clearly expressed. Carter, too, has regard for precedents – the windows in his 'Noah's Ark' were inspired by the *oeil de boeuf* openings of the Petit Trianon at Versailles – but his object's animal context adds point to the ox-eye pun.

His attitude to Nature is implied rather than stated. So it is with many Modernists. But what has changed, and changed frequently throughout the history of the furnished landscape, is the definition of Nature, and the employment of those making the definitions. Where architects and philosophers and painters once boldly discussed Nature's physical forms, and decided how they might be altered and represented, now it is as likely to be land artists and ecologists proclaiming Nature as sacred and ineffable. Unsurprisingly, Carter, who dislikes the post-Picturesque attitude to Nature, is also fierce about "half-baked ideas about what is Natural". The notion of the Picturesque is still with us, though diluted now to refer to real elements that would make an interesting picture. The conventions for 'interesting' are still with us, too. They are: variety and irregularity – not imitated, but selected and arranged to reinforce the general pictorial idea. It led on to more heroic ideas about Nature – the concept of the Sublime, the Romantic Movement, and so on to the present day, still susceptible to 'half-baked ideas'.

George Carter has knowingly sidestepped these post-Picturesque traditions. Well aware of late-twentieth-century issues in his chosen area, yet he prefers to address them with some deliberated archaisms, although these are – if you look carefully – in elegant quotation marks.

Cambridge, Ditchburn Place
Gardens: water feature by Mark
Chaimowicz, 1991. Glasswalling
supported by steel supports. Water
feature cast in concrete. Bench of
galvanised steel and marine ply.
Commissioned by Cambridge City
Council with financial assistance by
Eastern Arts Association.
Photograph: Reproduced by
permission of Cambridge City
Council, taken by Stephen P Rayment

Gateshead, National Garden
Festival: *Mythical Beast* play
structure by David Swift, 1990.
Wood with non-toxic stains and
paints, 261 × 240 × 72cms.
Commissioned by 'Festival
Landmarks' National Garden
Festival 1990 Ltd.
Photograph: Harriet McDougall

Basingstoke Hospital, children's
play court: maquette for 'Noah's
Ark' by George Carter, 1989.
Commissioned by Basingstoke
and Hampshire Health Authority.
Painted wood and plywood,
46cm × 51cm.
Photograph: George Carter

LOUISE SCULLION   Environmental Art is what she studied in
Glasgow – Art beyond the Gallery – art elsewhere. Now she is a nursing
assistant in the Department of Art Therapy in the Royal Cornhill Hospital
in Aberdeen. Before that she was Artist-in-Residence for eighteen months
– in the same hospital. By her own account, she is only just beginning to fit
in now, to learn how to fit in, as she finds herself to be a strange animal
within the hospital, searching for ways to make sense of what seems to her
like a very strange hotel.

As a maker of things, she became fascinated by the different natures of
treatment and illness. Art Therapy, Chemical Therapy; restorative modes
of activity operating within the broad themes of illness. Her own interest
seemed to be a social as well as a sympathetic appraisal of illness seen in
two ways: as closely observed behaviour; as a judgement by society. As an
artist, her interest in illness grew when she began to realize that it does not
have any boundaries. Possibly it exceeds, even might erase, the categories
and hierarchies that have been constructed to contain it; such as a hospital.

The making of objects seemed pushed to the edge of her speculations –
except as a portrayal of how individuals might choose to behave in this
environment. She described the old allotments, dating from the time when
the hospital had grown its own vegetables from the labour of able-bodied
patients. There were old beds and frames used as supports and dividers,
and green filing-cabinet drawers as plant boxes. In the middle, nearly
invisible, a chair. She kept her eye on it. It moved; from day to day it
became a sign of otherness, of unregulated, surreptitious action.

Her own chairs grew from that. 'Hannah and Mary' are similar but not
identical chairs (Hannah has arms) made in mild steel. They share certain
graphic qualities with Saul Steinberg's cartoons; a wary, wiry stance. In
addition, her chairs are joined together, with a single wiry strut; a kind of
mutual leash, as though each was taking the other for a walk. Their place
in an outdoor plaza is reached through a Scullion pergola of linked arches;
it's hung with painted panels that can be read as decoration, or, to do with
that novel of psychiatry, 'The White Hotel'. They are portrayals;
displaced portraits – part memorial, part miming by artefact, an object-
maker's mute eloquence. She remembers them well – her sitters, you
would have to call them – an unlikely, but finally firm, pair of friends.

JON MILLS   The furnished landscape is animated by movement and change, coming to life as people get involved with its structures, but also signalling to them about other powers – as windmills and waterwheels still do. The on-going metalwork by Jon Mills at the London Borough of Croydon's new library includes the weather-vane (the maquette is shown here) which crisply quotes two other kinds of roof-topping wind-worked mechanisms, the flag and the chimney cowl. His flag is a still image of wind-blown flutter; it is the pointing vane; it will be deep red. The flag's emblem will be gold – a cowl-like globe of fifteen fins that can spin to a glittering blur, or sparkle idly as a texture of S-shaped blades.

Mills's imagination works through a layering of emblems and devices – an accessible heraldry which happily mixes metaphors, as in the flag–ventilator–vane, and modes of representation. His steel banner, which hangs from an outside balcony on the library's third floor, repeats his flag's metal-formed static flutter, but has its own abilities to waver and ripple in the wind. Made in five sections, each independently swinging from stainless-steel rods, with phosphor-bronze bushes and grease nipples to make it nearly maintenance-free and – to his regret – silent.

In the children's library he has used a glass wall interspersed with columns as an armature for his coloured steel trees (which will be hung about with metal things of the children's own devising) and a connecting river of undulating railings with shoals of touchable, moveable metal fish. The trees, made to be looked up into, are topped by mirrors that will place the observer in the midst of those object-hung branches.

His work will appear throughout the library; sometimes as active ornament, sometimes so secretly placed that he hopes the visitor may notice a leaf, or a bird, only after the library has become a familiar place. The animation in his work is as much a matter of mood as of movement, although the mobility element is important because it suggests use: play and work, toy and tool, the mingling of associations and the layering of meanings which infuse these objects with a sense of friendly practicality.

Croydon, New Library: Maquette of weathervane by Jon Mills, 1991. Steel, 31cm. Commissioned by London Borough of Croydon. Photograph: Andrew Dunsmore

Aberdeen, Royal Cornhill Hospital,
courtyard: two chairs for Mary and
Hannah by Louise Scullion, 1991.
Mild steel. Commissioned by Royal
Cornhill Hospital, Aberdeen.
Photograph: Louise Scullion

OPPOSITE
Oxfordshire, Burford School:
maquette of weathervane by Jon
Mills for the school, 1992.
Mild steel. Commissioned by
Oxfordshire County Council.
Photograph: Rob Judges

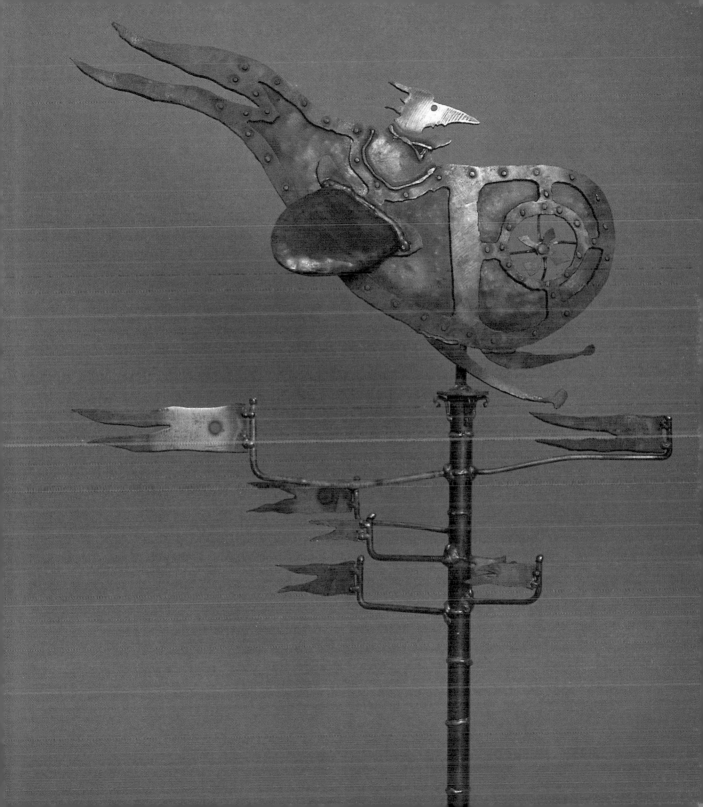

RICHARD LA TROBE-BATEMAN   Most of western Europe is a man-made landscape, as built as a palace or a cowshed. Such worked-over ground is alive with meanings; every physical where, as soon as it has been psychologically framed and focussed for us by a sympathetic culture, can become our special place.

La Trobe-Bateman is a passionate Modernist: an advocate in words, drawings and materials who argues his objects into existence. For him, Modernism is a matter of deep belief, not chosen style. Consequently, each place is viewed as a site for new action, based on formal analysis of need, revealed through a rational vision of what is possible. The special nature of each place, even for a maker as sensitive as he is to the pressures of historical forms, is discovered through that vision, through that problem-setting, problem-solving reading of circumstance. In fact, his bridges are the most conspicuous two-way interpretation of that process: the interchange between the real stuff of wood, steel, earth, water and weather, and the equally real forces of tension, compression, thrust, balance – and imagination.

There is a resonance, more technical and social than visual, that keeps his objects deliberately remote from the classic languages of architecture and furniture. When the physical and the conceptual logics fit each other, the artefact becomes a theorem displayed in diagrammatic form. But . . . And the 'but' is his inescapable sympathy and knowledge concerning related structures: all those shelters and props, barns and bridges, and the endless list of lesser things at the bottom of each age's cultural hierarchy. All the unshowy constructions whose prime meaning was their use.

As he says, "In furniture the questions are not so adrenalin-producing; with bridges the game really is out in the open." The Modernist principle of economy, so often expressed as Mies's "Less is more", but even more poignant as 'Almost nothing', is put to work in La Trobe-Bateman's bridges. He sees them as space diagrams – made subtle and daring by the qualities of his chosen materials: the oak, strong in compression; the steel wire, strong in tension. But each is weak if put to the other's test. The equation must be exact. But even when the bridge is in place, with all its forces balanced out – even then, he is delighted to confess, the crossing should still be a slight adventure.

PAUL DE MONCHAUX   A massive bench: one of four, all made to the same design, but formed from different stones with different geological ages. This bench, made from St Bees sandstone, is set on a pavement of the same stuff which has a carved description, "Triassic 250 million years old". Why? Sharing form, but not identity, although evidently made with a shared purpose in mind, some knowledge of the intention seems essential in order to interpret these objects. It is possible, even plausible, to place them in that High Victorian tradition of exemplary, didactic, educational, incontrovertible evidence of . . . something or other. But, no.

Perhaps this object's problematic function and relative status is intentional? A mute history of things? Paul de Monchaux, speaking as a sculptor, has plenty to say about the relations between making and meaning, between intention and speculation. The four benches share the theme of Time. Together, as they first were at the Gateshead Garden Festival in 1990, their specific material differences encouraged people to sense time aesthetically, as well as symbolically. As such, they remain close to the Victorian tableau previously prepared. But their rôle in the landscape is more evocative than that. De Monchaux speaks about the resonant influence of light on these landscape objects; light changing throughout each day, each year. His benches were tests for this influence. For sensitive observers, as for the maker, light can be the animator. In recent years he has learnt that the passage of light is an event with more active consequences than even the internal structure of the object it moves upon. All this is illuminated landscape; objects made to be seen in the searching light of metaphor and metaphysic. Symbolism is unavoidable, although de Monchaux suggests that symbols arrive in a work through an operation as random as the weather. He is less concerned about the physical climate and asserts that it is the changing cultural weather which shapes meaning by letting it gather slowly around things. This is the richer space of gradual experience. Within such space, work becomes a landmark, rather than a monument; is a place, rather than a thing. As the sculptor says, "If you want to speculate about something, then it has a history, and that's what sculpture is about."

Bridge by Richard La Trobe-
Bateman photographed over River
Alham, Somerset, 1989. Green oak
and stainless steel, 9.15m span.
Photograph: George Wright

Gateshead, National Garden
Festival: Bench by Paul de Monchaux,
1990. St. Bees Sandstone,
213.5 × 45.5 × 45.5cms.
Commissioned by British Rail
Community Unit.
Photograph: Reuben Kench

London, Homerton Hospital:
Optimistic Jug in construction by
Kate Malone, 1991. 'T' material,
earthenware fired. Commis-
sioned by Homerton Hospital
Arts Committee.
Photograph: Karen Robinson

Art and Craft Commissioning Information and contacts

Advice and help in a number of forms is available to organisations and individuals interested in commissioning art or craft work. Start by contacting one of the arts organisations listed below.

An up-to-date list of information resources including slide indexes, publications, public art organisations and public art agencies/consultants can be obtained from the Crafts Council (address below).

Arts Council of Great Britain
14 Great Peter Street
London SW1P 3NQ
Tel: 071 333 0100

Arts Council of Northern Ireland
181a Stranmillis Road
Belfast BT9 5DU
Tel: 0232 381591

Scottish Arts Council
12 Manor Place
Edinburgh EH3 7DD
Tel: 031 226 6051

Welsh Arts Council
Museum Place
Cardiff CF1 3NX
Tel: 0222 394711

The Crafts Council
44a Pentonville Road
London N1 9BY
Tel: 071 278 7700

Eastern Arts
Cherry Hinton Hall
Cherry Hinton Road
Cambridge CB1 4DW
Tel: 0223 215355

East Midlands Arts
Mountfields House
Forest Road
Loughborough
Leicestershire LE11 3HU
Tel: 0509 218292

London Arts Board
Elme House
133 Long Acre
London WC2E 9AS
Tel: 071 240 1313

North Wales Arts
10 Wellfield House
Bangor
Gwynedd LL57 1ER
Tel: 0248 353248

North West Arts
12 Harter Street
Manchester M1 6HY
Tel: 061 228 3062

Northern Arts
9–10 Osborne Terrace
Newcastle upon Tyne
NE2 1NZ
Tel: 091 281 6334

South East Arts
10 Mount Ephraim
Tunbridge Wells
Kent TN4 8AS
Tel: 0892 515210

South East Wales Arts
Victoria Street
Cwmbran
Gwent NP44 3YT
Tel: 0633 875075

South West Arts
Bradninch Place
Gandy Street
Exeter EX4 3LS
Tel: 0392 218188

Southern Arts
13 St Clement Street
Winchester
Hampshire SO23 9DQ
Tel: 0962 855099

West Midlands Arts
82 Granville Street
Birmingham B1 2LH
Tel: 021 631 3121

West Wales Arts
Dark Gate
3 Red Street
Carmarthen
Dyfed SA31 1QL
Tel: 0267 234248

Yorkshire & Humberside Arts
21 Bond Street
Dewsbury WF13 1AX
Tel: 0924 455555

Other contacts

The Landscape Institute
6–7 Barnard Mews
London SW11 1QU
Tel: 071 738 9166

**Royal Institute of
British Architects**
66 Portland Place
London W1N 4D1
Tel: 071 580 5533

Urban Design Group
8 Crinan Street
London N1 9SQ
Tel: 071 239 7777

**Art and Craft Commissioning
Selected reading list**

Art and Architecture
a handbook on commissioning
ed. Deanna Petherbridge
published by HMSO

Art and Craft Works
*a step-by-step guide from
Southern Arts*
13 St Clement Street
Winchester
Hampshire SO23 9DQ

Art for Public Places
critical essays
ed. Malcolm Miles
published by Winchester School of
Art Press, Park Avenue, Winchester
Hampshire

Art Within Reach
ed. Peter Townsend
Published by Thames & Hudson
30 Bloomsbury Street
London WC1B 3QP

**Lewisham: a plan for involving
art in the town centre**
by John Maine
published by the London Borough
of Lewisham

Memorials by Artists
Harriet Frazer
Shape Priory
Saxmundham
Suffolk
IP17 1SA

New Milestones
sculpture, community & the land
by Joanna Morland
published by Common Ground
45 Shelton Street
London WC2H 9HJ

Percent for Art: a Review
ed. Alan Haydon
and Isabel Vasseur
Published by the Arts Council
14 Great Peter Street, London
SW1P 3NQ

The Public Art Report
*local authority commissions of art
for public places*
by Phyllida Shaw
published by Public Art Forum
c/o PADT, 1A Cobham Mews
Agar Grove, London NW1 9SB

INDEX

Listing contemporary British makers
included in this book
Figures in *italic* refer to illustrations